LYNDON HILLING
WALTER BERGMANN

Second Book of Bassoon Solos

Zweites Spielbuch für Fagott

Dedicated to Greta Bergmann

Faber Music Limited
London

Bärenreiter-Verlag, Kassel : Boosey & Hawkes (Australia) Pty. Ltd., Sydney
Boosey & Hawkes (Canada) Ltd., Willowdale : G. Schirmer Inc., New York

© 1981 by Faber Music Ltd
First published in 1981 by Faber Music Ltd
3 Queen Square London WC1N 3AU
Music drawn by Michael Rowe
Cover design by Shirley Tucker
Printed in England by Caligraving Ltd

Contents

Preface

This second book of bassoon solos is designed for the bassoon student in the second or third year of learning. The pieces cover a wide variety of styles and aim to explore the expressive qualities of the instrument. They are arranged in chronological order, not according to difficulty, and there are brief explanatory notes.

The editors would like to thank Martin Kingsbury and Malcolm Tyler for their help in preparing this volume.

L. H.
W. B.

1. SINFONIA

JOHANN SEBASTIAN BACH
(1685–1750)

2. ARIA

JOHANN SEBASTIAN BACH
(1685-1750)

3. MARCH

GEORGE FRIDERIC HANDEL
(1685-1759)

4. GAVOTTE

GEORGE FRIDERIC HANDEL
(1685-1759)

5. L'HIVER

GEORG PHILIPP TELEMANN
(1681-1767)

Bassoon part

LYNDON HILLING
WALTER BERGMANN

Second Book of
Bassoon Solos

Zweites Spielbuch
für Fagott

Dedicated to Greta Bergmann

Faber Music Limited
London

Bärenreiter-Verlag, Kassel : Boosey & Hawkes (Australia) Pty. Ltd., Sydney
Boosey & Hawkes (Canada) Ltd., Willowdale : G. Schirmer Inc., New York

Contents

© 1981 by Faber Music Ltd
First published in 1981 by Faber Music Ltd
3 Queen Square London WC1N 3AU
Music drawn by Michael Rowe
Cover design by Shirley Tucker
Printed in England by Caligraving Ltd
All rights reserved

Preface

This second book of bassoon solos is designed for the bassoon student in the second or third year of learning. The pieces cover a wide variety of styles and aim to explore the expressive qualities of the instrument. They are arranged in chronological order, not according to difficulty, and there are brief explanatory notes.

The editors would like to thank Martin Kingsbury and Malcolm Tyler for their help in preparing this volume.

L. H.
W. B.

1. SINFONIA

JOHANN SEBASTIAN BACH
(1685-1750)

1. Bach's church cantatas contain some of his finest music. This sinfonia (scored for oboe, strings and basso continuo) is the introduction to Cantata No. 156. Bach also used it as the slow movement of his Harpsichord Concerto in F minor. Long, well-shaped phrases and good breath control are needed here. In bar 9 relax the embouchure and half-hole carefully for a good top A flat.

In Bachs Kirchenkantaten steckt ein guter Teil seiner besten Kompositionen. Die Sinfonia (im Original für Oboe, Streichorchester und basso continuo) ist die Einleitung zu Kantate Nr. 156. Bach benutzte sie auch als langsamen Satz des Cembalokonzertes in f moll. Die langen melodischen Phrasen verlangen gute Atemkontrolle. In Takt 9 werden lockerer Ansatz und Kontrolle des Halbloches für das hohe As benötigt.

2. ARIA

JOHANN SEBASTIAN BACH
(1685-1750)

2. In baroque music the bass line — the basso continuo — was of special importance. It was the foundation for the upper parts and indicated the harmony to the keyboard player. In this arrangement of an aria for bass voice, three oboes and basso continuo from Cantata No. 26, the bassoon plays the continuo in the opening and da capo sections but takes over the vocal line in the middle.

Für die Musik des Barock war die Bassstimme—der "basso continuo"—von besonderer Bedeutung. Sie war das Fundament der darüber liegenden Stimmen und wies dem Cembalospieler die zu findenden Harmonien an. In unserm Arrangement spielt das Fagott im ersten und letzten ("da capo") Teil der Arie die Continuo–, im Mittelteil die Gesangsstimme. Das Original ist eine Bassarie mit 3 Oboen und basso continuo aus Kantate Nr. 26.

3. MARCH

GEORGE FRIDERIC HANDEL
(1685-1759)

3 & 4. These two lively pieces are taken from Handel's Trio Sonata for two violins and continuo, op. 5. They should be played with neat tongueing and crisp rhythm. In this period trills usually start on the upper note.

Diese zwei lebhaften Stücke sind Händels Triosonaten für zwei Violinen und basso continuo op.5 entnommen. Gute Artikulation und präziser Rhythmus werden erfordert. Zu Händels Zeiten fing man Triller mit der oberen Note an.

6

4. GAVOTTE

GEORGE FRIDERIC HANDEL
(1685-1759)

5. L'HIVER

GEORG PHILIPP TELEMANN
(1681-1767)

5. Telemann produced a music magazine, *Der getreue Music-Meister,* containing solos for all the popular instruments of the day. 'Winter' is a short descriptive piece designed 'for any instrument'. This exquisite melody requires good legato tongueing.

Telemann gab eine Musikzeitschrift "Der getreue Music-Meister" heraus, die Stücke für alle damals gebräuchlichen Instrumente enthielt. "Winter", ein "Galanterie" Stück, war "pour divers instruments" bestimmt. Die erlesene Melodie verlangt gutes Binden ("legato").

6. LARGO

FRANCESCO BARSANTI
(*c.*1690-1772)

6. Barsanti was born and trained in Italy, but in 1714 emigrated to Britain and settled in London as a professional woodwind, later viola, player. In this Largo, taken from the Sonata in C for treble recorder and continuo, the bassoon plays the continuo line while the recorder part is transferred to the upper line of the piano. The tempo should not be too slow; a gently flowing three beats in a bar.

Barsanti wurde in Italien geboren und erzogen. 1717 ging er nach England und liess sich in London als Holzblas-instrumentspieler (später als Bratschist) nieder. Das Largo ist der dritte Satz seiner Sonate in C für Blockflöte und basso continuo. In unserem Arrangement ist die Continuostimme dem Fagott, die Blockflötenstimme dem Klavier zugeteilt. Das Tempo darf nicht zu langsam genommen werden: drei gemächliche Schläge pro Takt.

7. AIR

JOHANN CHRISTIAN SCHICKHARDT
(c.1682-1762)

7. This air is taken from the sixth sonata of Schick-hardt's '24 sonatas in all keys' op. 30 (1735). Think in two beats rather than four beats in a bar. The figure ♫. in bars 4, 12 and 22 should be played gently and not exaggerated.

Die "Air" ist der 6. Sonate von Schickhardts "24 Sonaten in allen Tonarten" op. 30 (1735) entnommen. Das Zeitmass soll halbtaktig, nicht in 4 Vierteln genommen werden. Der Vorschlag ♫. in den Takten 4, 12 und 22 ist ruhig, nicht überakzentuiert zu spielen.

8

8. THE MAIDEN'S BLUSH *or* BUMP HER BELLY

English Country Dance
(1719)

8. This set of free variations is based on a tune found in volume 2 of *The Dancing Master* (third edition, 1719), the famous collection of English country dance tunes. Here is an opportunity for the bassoonist to play with vigour and to make the most of the humorous qualities of the instrument. Bars 34-7 will need slow practice to ensure even quavers and the correct use of the half-hole and speaker keys.

Dies sind freie Variationen einer Melodie aus "The Dancing Master", einer berühmten Sammlung englischer Tänze aus dem Jahre 1719. Sie geben dem Fagottisten Gelegenheit, die robusten und humoristischen Seiten seines Instruments zu zeigen. Die Takte 34–37 verlangen langsames Üben der Achtelpassagen und richtigen Gebrauch des Halbloches und der Oktavklappen.

9. ALLEGRO CON SPIRITO

JOHANN CHRISTIAN BACH
(1735-1782)

10

9. Johann Christian Bach, the youngest son of Johann Sebastian, came to London in 1763 where he became the Queen's composer. Mozart was greatly influenced by his music. This Allegro is a transcription of the first movement of the sonata op. 16, no. 5 for 'Harpsichord or Piano-Forte with an Accompaniment for a German Flute or Violin'. The bassoon and the piano are of equal importance, so both players must decide where they have the solo line and where they are accompanying.

Johann Christian Bach, jüngster Sohn Johann Sebastians, kam 1763 nach London, wo er Komponist der Königin wurde. Mozart war sehr beeinflusst von seiner Musik. Das Allegro ist eine Transskription des ersten Satzes der Sonate op. 17 Nr. 5 für "Cembalo oder Pianoforte mit Begleitung einer Flöte oder Violine". Fagott und Klavier sind musikalisch von gleicher Bedeutung, beide Spieler müssen sich deshalb klarmachen, ob sie Melodie oder Begleitung spielen.

10. PRELUDE

FRANZ JOSEPH HAYDN
(1732-1809)

10, 11 & Haydn's employer, Prince Esterhazy, played the
12. baryton, a stringed instrument now obsolete, for which Haydn wrote more than a hundred trios with viola or violin and bass. These are the sources of the three movements which may be played separately or as a group. The Adagio explores the middle register of the bassoon. Relax the embouchure and use plenty of air to produce sonorous bottom notes. In the Minuet, bars 9-13, do not hit the second beat of each bar too hard but follow on from the piano. In the *minore* section of the Finale be prepared for the change of key and use a small half-hole to help the A flats to speak clearly.

Haydns Arbeitgeber, Fürst Esterhazy, spielte Baryton, ein heute nicht mehr gebräuchliches Streichinstrument, für das Haydn mehr als 100 Trios mit Bratsche oder Violine oder Bass schrieb. Die Stücke Nr. 10–12 sind diesen Trios entnommen; sie können einzeln oder als Gruppe gespielt werden. Das Adagio beutet die Mittellage des Fagotts aus. Der Spieler muss den Ansatz entspannen und viel Luft gebrauchen, um klangvolle, tiefe Töne zu erzeugen. Im Menuet, Takt 9–13, soll er vermeiden, den zweiten Taktteil zu betonen, vielmehr dem Klavier folgen. Im Mollteil des Finales sei er auf den Tonartenwechsel vorbereitet und gebrauche ein schmales Halbloch für ein klares Mittel-As.

11. MENUET

FRANZ JOSEPH HAYDN
(1732 - 1809)

Menuet da capo

12. FINALE

FRANZ JOSEPH HAYDN
(1732 - 1809)

13. ARIA: 'DALLA SUA PACE'

from *Don Giovanni*

WOLFGANG AMADEUS MOZART
(1756-1791)

13. The source of this piece is a tenor aria from Mozart's opera *Don Giovanni* in a contemporary transcription for wind octet by Johann Triebensee, director and teacher of the Royal Imperial Court Theatre Wind Ensemble. Such arrangements of well-known pieces for wind ensemble were very popular. A warm, singing tone and a little well-judged rubato are needed to make the most of this lovely melody.

Die Quelle dieser Tenorarie aus Mozarts Don Giovanni ist eine zeitgenössische Transskription für Bläseroktett von Johann Triebensee, Direktor des Bläserensembles und Lehrer am Kaiserlichen Hoftheater in Wien. Solche Arrangements bekannter Stücke für Bläserensembles waren derzeit sehr beliebt. Ein warmer, singender Ton und ein vorsichtiges Rubato werden der herrlichen Melodie am besten gerecht.

14. LARGHETTO

ANTONIN DVOŘÁK
(1841-1904)

14. In 1893, while staying in America, Dvořák composed a Sonatina for violin and piano, op. 100, and dedicated it to his six children. This is a slightly shortened arrangement of the second movement of the work. Take great care over the dynamics, starting quite firmly so that a real contrast can be made in bar 9.

Dvořák komponierte im Jahre 1893 während seines Aufenthalts in Amerika eine Sonatine (op.100) für Violine und Klavier und widmete sie seinen 6 Kindern. Das Larghetto ist der (leicht gekürzte) zweite Satz dieser Sonatine. Die Dynamik ist genau zu beachten. Der Anfang ist bestimmt zu spielen, um im Takt 9 den Kontrast deutlich herauszubringen.

15. ALBUM LEAF

EDVARD GRIEG
(1843-1907)

15. Grieg was a master of the miniature and produced numerous descriptive piano pieces. This 'Album Leaf', written in 1867, is taken from the first of his ten books of *Lyric Pieces*. In bar 2, and all similar places, play the grace note just before the beat and notice that the second quaver is not staccato.

Grieg war ein Meister der Kleinkunst; er schrieb zahlreiche Charakterstücke für Klavier. Das "Albumblatt", komponiert 1867, ist dem ersten Band seiner zehnbändigen "Lyrischen Stücke" entnommen. Der Vorschlag in Takt 2 und an allen gleichen Stellen muss kurz vor der nächsten Note gespielt werden. In den Takten 2–4 und an gleichen Stellen hat die zweite Note keinen staccato Punkt.

16. ANDALUZA

ENRIQUE GRANADOS
(1887-1916)

16. Granados was the father of modern Spanish piano music. His reputation as a composer rests largely on his *Spanish Dances* from which 'Andaluza' is taken. It must be played with great rhythmic flexibility in order to bring out the distinctive character of Spanish folk music.

Granados war der Vater der Spanischen Klaviermusik. Sein Ruf als Komponist beruht hauptsächlich auf seinen "Spanischen Tänzen", zu denen Andaluza gehört. Um den typischen Charakter der spanischen Volksmusik zu wahren, muss das Stück mit grosser rhythmischer Freiheit gespielt werden.

6. LARGO

FRANCESCO BARSANTI
(*c*.1690–1772)

7. AIR

JOHANN CHRISTIAN SCHICKHARDT
(*c.*1682-1762)

8. THE MAIDEN'S BLUSH *or* BUMP HER BELLY

English Country Dance (1719)

(Bump her belly)

9. ALLEGRO CON SPIRITO

JOHANN CHRISTIAN BACH
(1735-1782)

10. PRELUDE

FRANZ JOSEPH HAYDN
(1732 - 1809)

11. MENUET

FRANZ JOSEPH HAYDN
(1732 – 1809)

12. FINALE

FRANZ JOSEPH HAYDN
(1732 - 1809)

13. ARIA: 'DALLA SUA PACE'

from *Don Giovanni*

WOLFGANG AMADEUS MOZART
(1756-1791)

14. LARGHETTO

ANTONIN DVOŘÁK
(1841-1904)

15. ALBUM LEAF

EDVARD GRIEG
(1843-1907)

Con pedale

16. ANDALUZA

ENRIQUE GRANADOS
(1887-1916)